Website Building

How to Build your Own Website and Blog to Perfection!

Malcolm Rockwood

ISBN: 1515302652
ISBN-13: 978-1515302650

DEDICATION

To my Father and to all of those moments I wanted to fall into despair only to pick myself back up and start walking again.

CONTENTS

ACKNOWLEDGMENTS

Everyone seems to think that the D.N.S system is a big deal, but it's not the heartbeat of the Internet. Who controls the flow of the ocean? Nobody controls it, and it works just fine. There are some things that can't be controlled and should be left distributed.

Leonard Kleinrock

1 INTRODUCTION

I want to thank you and congratulate you for buying the book, "Website Building: How to Build your Own Website and Blog to Perfection!"

This book contains proven steps and strategies on how to create your very own website, web page, and blog. Most people get intimidated by all the technical details and terms involved with the process. Fortunately, this book will help you go through each step. You will learn:

- What websites, web pages, and blogs are all about

- What are domains, domain names, and web hosts

- Tips on how to choose the best domain names and domain registrars

- Information about the different web hosts and types of web hosts

- What are the best platforms available

- And so much more!

Thanks again for buying this book, I hope you enjoy it!

2 HISTORY OF THE INTERNET

The history of the Internet can be traced back all the way to the 1950's with the invention and the development of the first electric computer. It is impossible to credit one person for the invention of the Internet; it took many people working together cohesively to create the entity known as the Internet. The primary motivation for the creation of the Internet came from the Soviet Union. Leaders in America were concerned that if the Soviet Union were to launch missiles at us and just one of them was able to hit the nations primary hub of lines and wires that made long-distance communications possible, then the resulting chaos would be detrimental. After the Soviet Union launched the first satellite, known as "Sputnik" America went into overdrive.

The federal government created an agency known as the Department of Defense's Advanced Research Projects Agency, or ARPA for short, and their goal was to match the speed of the Soviet union and develop technologies that can be used in space. In 1962 there was a scientist by the name of J.C.R. Licklider who proposed a solution for the problem of a missile hitting our wire hubs: a nationwide network of computers that would be able to talk to each other. This network would, in theory, allow the leaders of the American government to talk to each other in the scenario of the Soviet Union destroying our telephone system.

A few years later in 1965, a scientist from M.I.T., named Leonard Kleinrock, developed a way of sending information from computer to computer by using a method called "packet switching". Traditionally the first "Internet", also known as ARPAnet, was a network of four computers connected to each other and was only able to send and receive long threads of information. Packet Switching allowed the messages to break down into small pockets of information, or data, and each packet would take its own route to the destination in the network.

This is where things get really exciting. From just those four computers the network began to grow with the addition of more computers. In 1971 ARPAnet added another network to its own, the network from the University of Hawaii (fondly known as ALOHAnet). Two years later ARPAnet became worldwide with the addition of two more networks: the London's University College network and the Royal Radar Establishment network in Norway. One thing to remember is that these computers in all of these networks were all packet-switched computers and the more computers that was added to the network the more difficult it began to integrate them all into a single entity that would later be called the Internet.

Another scientist stepped forward with the solution and his name was Vinton Cerf. Vinton came up with a new protocol, or method of instructions, within the computer network. This method would allow each computer, no matter where it was in the network, to talk to another computer. This invention was called the Transmission Control Protocol, or TCP for short. It is also important to know that he would later develop another protocol known as the Internet Protocol. This is why we refer to this uniform protocol today as TCP/IP. Another term you may have heard in reference to this protocol is "the handshake" which describes the distant computers being introduced in virtual space.

The TCP/IP protocol transformed the network into a worldwide network and throughout the 1970's and 80's scientists and researchers used it to send data from one computer to another. This wasn't the final form of the Internet, and its final form came from a computer programmer named Tim Berners-Lee. He introduced the true form of the World Wide Web; a form of the Internet that was more than a simple way of sending information from one place to another but a place or "web" of information that can be retrieved by anyone connected to the Internet. Everything that you have done with the Internet from looking at video files of cats, researching information for school, or simply looking up an article about how to cook a cake from scratch can all be done by Tim Bernes-Lee.

However the method of finding this information was blocky, hard to heard, and obviously mean for people who had the education to understand the Internet. In 1992 a group of researchers and students from the University of Illinois developed a "browser" that they called the Mosaic, which would later become known as Netscape. The use of this browser was to make using the Internet more user-friendly. The browser did this by allowing users to see the words and pictures all on the same page as well as allowing the user to navigate using links that you could click on that would take you to another place within the Internet.

From that moment on the Internet exploded with commerce. Companies realized that they could post information about their business on the World Wide Web. More companies began to realize that they could even sell their goods directly to customers without ever actually having to physically talk to them or see them. In later years social network sites, like Facebook and Twitter, would allow people to always stay connected no matter where they were at in the world.

One key thing to understand is that even though the "Internet" isn't a physical entity that you can touch it is a form of technology and is always changing. Scientists, researchers, and programmers are discovering ways to send information faster. Ways are being developed and implemented that are making the computers themselves more efficient in power and in speed. The Internet that we know of right now may not be the same as it will be in ten, fifty, or a hundred years from now.

3 WEBSITE 101

A web page refers to the individual pages of a certain website. For example, the Home, About Us, and FAQ are the web pages. A website is basically a collection of several web pages.

WEBSITES

Types

There are numerous kinds of websites on the Internet. Here are just some of the mist common types:

Organization Website

This includes websites for organizations, groups, communities, or churches. These sites are put up in order to provide information about the group. This type of website is often used as a means of sending updates to members. It is also used to spread awareness about the group's vision and mission.

Business Websites

This type of website is most often used to provide product information. Some business websites use this to promote new and upcoming products. This is also a good platform to advertise the business, reaching a wider market. Most businesses also find putting up business websites as a less costly means of advertising their products and services than other types of marketing and advertising methods.

Hobby Websites

These are websites where one can learn about different kinds of crafts, learn new tricks, find tips, or share experiences about hobbies. Examples are websites about fishing, where tips on how to catch particular fish species, where to fish, weather updates, and other related topics.

Some hobby websites focus on just proving tips and information. Some use these sites to offer products and services. Some use both, using either products or tips to draw website visitors.

Money-making Websites

A type of website that is continually growing in popularity is the money-generating type. This website type helps people to make money online.

4 DOMAIN NAME AND WEB HOST

When setting up a website, you will be asked for a domain name and look for a web host. These 2 are the most basic steps you need to take before you can proceed with your website design.

DOMAIN NAME

The domain name is much like a specific address that will allow internet users to know where to find you (your website, that is). For example, in an internet address *http://www.example.com/index.html*, the domain name is *example.com*.

Domain names have a TDL or top level domain. This refers to pretty much what category a website is. For the sample above (*http://www.example.com/index.html*), the TDL is *.com*. There are a limited number of TDLs used in setting up a website. The following are the most common ones:

- **.gov** – domain names used for websites of government agencies

- **.mil** – used for official websites of military agencies and units

- **.edu** – educational institutions

- **.org** – used for websites on non-profit organizations

- **.com** – used for websites of commercial business

- **.net** – used for websites of network organizations

Countries and states also use their standard abbreviations in the TDL, such as:

- **.ca** - Canada

- **.th** – Thailand

- **.ph** – Philippines

- **.fl** – Florida

Why Get Domain Names

It is highly advisable to register the domain name when putting up a website.

Domain names are important because it helps in tracking down or directing Internet users to your website. Website visitors can still follow you even if you changed your webhost (more on Web hosting later). Regular visitors (or those who are interested in your website) can simply type the domain name into the address bar and they will automatically be directed to your site. The domain name also gives credibility to the website. For example, a *.org* domain name gives the impression that the organization is legit. The domain name is also very helpful for business and money-generating websites. Statistics reveal that most people are likely to do business with a website that has its own domain name compared to ones that don't.

Having your own domain name also puts label to your website. Visitors get an idea of what your website is all about just by your URL or web address. For example, you post a link to your website, with *.com* domain name, in one of your ads. By just looking at your site domain, they'd know the site has something about business.

It would be much easier for people to remember your site, too. To make it more recognizable and easier to remember, make the domain name as (yourproduct/company).com. For example, use a domain name babybibs.com or gardentools.com. This way, people who would be typing "baby bibs" or "garden tools" in the search bar would most likely be directed to your site.

Another advantage of having your own domain name is more advertisers. Your website has an aura of respectability, which exudes trust and confidence. More sponsors would be willing to advertise your website.

How to register your domain name

Registering domain names may or may not require a fee. This depends on your web host. A registrar is available online where you can register your domain name, pay a few fees and then you have the right to use that particular domain for a year. You will be required to renew the registration annually.

Some web hosts will do the registration for you. Some may even pay the required fees and offer the domain name to you for free. This offer is most often found in web hosting sites that cater to commercial websites. Some web hosts may do the registration but you have to pay the fees.

The advantage of registering your domain name directly to a registrar assures you that you are the legitimate owner of that name. You also get to register yourself as the technical and the administrative contact. When relying on web hosts for the registration, most often, the web host would be listed as the contact and not you. Being the registered owner and contact may later prove very important. You may want to have a 100% control on your domain, so it is advisable to do the registration yourself though there are some web hosts that may charge ridiculously high fees to allow you to continue using that domain name.

You should also make sure you are the registered owner and not the web host so you can have better control on what happens to the site. For example, before your website is removed from a web host, the registrar will have to obtain your approval first. Also, registering on your own ensures you get to register your preferred name as soon as possible, before someone else claims it.

To register:

- Think of a shortlist of names you want and rank them according to your preference. Rank your most favorite name first. This way, when you register and find out the name you like has already been taken, you can quickly go to the next name on your list.

- Registering on your own would require a fee. It generally ranges from US$4 to US$10. For this, you will either need a PayPal account or a credit card. By paying, you get to stake a claim on the domain name immediately.

- If you have already contacted a web host, ask them for their primary and secondary nameservers. This is often available on the FAQ page of your chosen webhost. Look under DNS, domain name or domain name transfer portion. If the information is not there, email the web host for the information. Primary and secondary nameservers are important because these will help point your domain name to the website you are creating.

- If you haven't decided on a web host yet, you have the option to park your domain name with the registrar. Your domain name will be set up in a temporary website that the registrar will make just for you. This allows you to set up your domain name and have the website out up before it become too late for you. This way, you also get to spend more time you need to focus on the other details of the website such designing and getting sponsors. A lot of registrars do this automatically, without requiring you to take any special step.

Domain Name Registrars You Can Use

You can use any registrar for your domain name. There are lots to choose from. Here are the more popular ones:

GoDaddy.com

This is the largest registrar in the world. It is the most popularly used and is considered one of the biggest. This registrar offers *.com* names for a relatively small fee. Additional fees are required if transferring from some other registrar.

GoDaddy offers its registrants web interface to help in managing the domain. There is also free web redirection, which allows visitors of your website to be transferred to another website you want to get redirected to. Other offers include a free starter, parked and/or "for sale" web page, and an option for a private registration where the domain name can be registered under a proxy company.

This registrar also offers the following domain names:

- **.com**

- **.biz**

- **.us**

- **.org**

- **.net**

- **.name**

- **.info**

- **.ws**

- **.tv**

- **.org.uk**

- **.co.uk**

- **.me.uk**

Prices vary depending on the type of domain being registered. Some domain names are more expensive than others. PayPal and credit card payments are accepted.

Namecheap

This is also one of the most widely used registrars with good offers. For a fee, your domain name registration comes with lots of freebies, such as email forwarding, web redirection (of your choice), and parking for the domain name.

For the 1st year upon registration, you can avail of the WhoisGuard, a feature that masks your domain particulars from public view. This feature is free.

Domain name extensions offered by this registrar include the following:

- **.org**

- **.net**

- **.info**

- **.biz**

- **.de**

- **.co**

- **.us**

- **.co.uk**

Payments are accepted from PayPal accounts or credit cards.

1&1 Internet

This is a domain name registrar as well as a web host. Offered domains include the following:

- **.net**

- **.org**

- **.us**

- **.com**

- **.info**

- **.biz**

The registration fee includes private registration for the domain. Private registration means the particulars are kept hidden from the public view. This is achieved by using a proxy company's name when registering the domain. Along with this are freebie like DNS management, email account, starter website and domain masking and forwarding. Payments are accepted through PayPal or credit cards.

Dotster.com

This is quite popular and provides domain registration at pretty inexpensive fees. The prices are even lower as the domain is a transfer from other registrars. Along with the registration, you can get a web interface that makes domain management more convenient. There is also an option to privately register the domain under a proxy company name. Domain names available through Dotster.com include:

- **.md**

- **.tv**

- **.info**

- **.biz**

- **.net**

- **.com**

- **.org**

- **.name**

- **.de**

- **.cc**

- **.ca**

- **.us**

- **.sr**

- **.us.com**

- .co.uk

Payments can be made through a PayPal account or credit card.

Aside from these, there are several more registrars available. Also, commercial web hosts can offer free domain names that you can choose from.

Choosing the Domain Name

Your domain name is as important as the rest of the others things to consider when creating a website. Here are a few guidelines to help you decide on a successful domain name:

- If the domain name is for a business website, it is most helpful if you put your company name in the domain. For example, choose your domain name as CompanyName.com such as "AngelCrafts.com", "FishingWorld.com", etc.

- If the website is a personal page, place YourName.com as your domain. For example, "AndyBucksworth.com", "AnnaPright.com". This is ideal for people who want to provide tips or updates in certain fields such as health and beauty.

- If the first 2 are not attractive for you, try these:

  o Brandable – If you want your site to become a brand or a household name in a certain field, choose a domain that promotes what the site is all about. For example, if your website is to feature awareness on cancer, good domain suggestions would be "cancerawareness.org" and "supportforbreastcancer.net".

  o Memorable – Most people won't memorize an entire string of web address. They are more attracted to domains that are short and memorable. Too long, fuzzy and makes no connection to what the site is all about are less likely to be memorable. For example, people would likely keep visiting the page with a domain "baseball.org" rather than a similar website with a domain"bsb1892746xhs.net"

o Catchy – Just as you would think of a catchy company and product name, so should your domain name be.

WEB HOSTING

A web host is a service provider that supports websites. This service allows a website to be available on the Internet, allowing other people to see the website and visit it anytime.

Web hosting services work by taking the files of your website and store it in high-powered type of computers that are connected with a fats-performing network. Once someone enters your website's address, the Internet will connect to the server that contains your website's files. It will transfer the information about your website back to the person's computer. The person who entered your website's address is now able to view the pages in your website.

Types

There are different types of web hosting, each designed to support the different website and customer needs. Types include shared web hosting, cloud hosting, website builder and dedicated hosting.

Shared Web Hosting

This is the most common web hosting service type. It is also known simply as web hosting or website hosting. Beginners at setting up their own websites would do well to start with this type because it is easiest to use. A shared web hosting is a type of service where many customers or users share one server.

Advantages of using shared web hosting include the following:

- Cheaper – This type of service is cheaper compared to other types. Some don't even require upfront payment. Also, the payment is minimal since many users are availing of the same services.

- Easier – Shared web hosting services come already preconfigured. Options and features that are most often asked for of the company are already preconfigured. Any security updates and maintenance issues are already handled by the company.

- Sharing – You can easily share the resources of the server with others who are also using the same web host.

While it does provide a lot of good and convenience, shared web hosting has its own disadvantages, too. Some of these are:

- Traffic – Since you are sharing the same server with a number of other users, your website might slow down as a result. This is especially true if one of the shared websites becomes very busy.

- Less flexibility – Joining a shared web host is much like living with others in an apartment block. There are some things you can't do because it may affect or inconvenience others. For example, you can't modify any of the core components or block any of the ports.

Website Builder

A website builder allows you to easily build your own website and get it online. It provides hundreds of templates with professional designs which you can choose from in order to build your website. These templates help you get started with your website. Some website builders also allow a few customizations to these templates to make it more unique and suit your preferences.

Website builders also come with a domain name for free. Web hosting account is also automatically set up for you.

There are advantages to choosing website builders for web hosting service needs. These include:

- Easy to get online – There is no additional learning or skills just to get you started on your website. The templates are a great help. These cut down most of the preliminary work for you, thus helping you get your website online in the soonest possible time.

- Low cost professional output – Getting a web designer to create your website may require a lot of time and would likely cost a good sum. With web builders, the templates are all made by experts, which ensure your website will look professionally done. Some web builders would only require a small monthly fee for the use o the templates. Some also allow you to edit your website anytime you want.

- Customizations – It may be difficult for most when dealing with complex customizations that involve HTML 5, scrolling or image display. There are different kinds of software in web builders that take care of these things for you.

Despite the attractive advantages, there are also some downsides to using web builders, such as:

- Tricky – Some businesses that are involved in large ecommerce activities may need a tailor-made website. The templates, although professionally done, may not cater to the more complex needs. Although, the web builder can still support the sale of services and products, it may not be able to keep up with the specific needs.

- Difficulty with more specialized customization – Web builders will allow you to change or embed codes. However, it will be difficult to deal with more complex changes.

Cloud Hosting

This is a combination of dedicated hosting and shared hosting, with a few unique features as well. Users of cloud hosting websites still share one physical server. The difference is the special virtualization technology partitions. These split up the physical server in the technological sense. This creates individual cloud servers that allow each user to have their own resources dedicated solely for their use. These individual serves can be configured much like a fully dedicated web host server.

Advantages of cloud hosting include the following:

- Flexibility – Users of cloud hosting receive the most flexibility possible in the world of web hosting. The cloud has the ability to adapt to any problems in the physical hardware. It also automatically puts your website in trustworthy and dependable location. When traffic is high, the cloud offers options for seamless and fast upgrades.

- Dedicated resources – websites on cloud hosting servers receive dedicated resources, which also includes dedicated CPU, memory and bandwidth. This means that even if you share the same server equipment, you have exclusive use of resources. This would prevent neighbors with higher traffic from using your resources and leaving you with slow function when you need them.

- Fewer sharing – Because of the individual servers within 1 physical server, there are fewer sharing and more resources for your exclusive use anytime.

- Freedom to configure – Because you get to have your own resources, you are free to make the modifications that you want. This is made possible by the virtualization software. This same software is also able to assume technical experience in higher levels.

Dedicated Hosting

This type of web hosting is considered the most reliable and most recommended. This type of hosting allows users to have their very own server, including all of its resources. The server is solely dedicated to your website. This is much like living in your own house and not in a building with several apartment units.

Advantages include the following:

- Customization and Flexibility – Users get to choose the exact specifications for the software and hardware to be used for their websites.

- Guaranteed performance and fully dedicated server resources – Everything is dependent on your website activity and not on anyone else's. That is, the speed depends on the traffic to your website, and not affected by the traffic of other websites.

- Full Control – Because the server is all yours, you have full access even to the root or the most basic parts. You can anything you want, tweak whatever parameters and components to suit your needs.

The main disadvantages are technical skill requirements and cost. This is definitely more expensive compared to other web hosting services. Also, you need to have technical knowledge and skills before you even use dedicated web hosts. Everything related to your website will be your own responsibility. You will need to solve any problems that may arise.

5 SETTING UP YOUR OWN WEBSITE

After registering the domain name and finding a web host, you can now proceed to setting up your own website.

BUILDING PLATFORM

The platform allows you to create your website. Before, like in 2004, most websites were built using CSS, FLASH, or HTML. Today, majority of the websites are made using CMS or Content Management Systems. Popular CMS include WordPress, Drupal, and Joomla, but majority of websites run on the WordPress platform.

WordPress

The advantages of using WordPress include the following:

- There's no need for prior knowledge on computer coding language such as HTML.

- This platform is free with different themes or layouts that you can choose from.

- This platform creates access to several users who are also allowed to publish content to the blog

- WordPress allows adding images, videos and content to the website by just logging in to the WordPress dashboard.

Website Building: How to Build your Own Website and Blog to Perfection!

- The website looks very professional with little effort and cost.

- The website works well on computers, laptops and other gadgets like tablets and mobile phones.

- The website can be set up and go online in under 30 minutes.

WordPress as a platform is the best for beginners because it is easy to learn, free, and very convenient. This is most recommended for small to medium-sized blogs and websites.

Drupal

This is the second most widely used website building platform today. This works well for websites dealing with ecommerce. However, users need to have some knowledge about technical encoding. This program is totally open-source. A good number of website builders prefer Drupal, especially those who already have some technical know-how.

This platform is exceptionally powerful. Compared to WordPress, Drupal is less intensive when it comes to resources. It can be set up for a wide range of applications, from simple blogs to content portals for big corporations.

A few of the best advantages when using Drupal include the following:

- Technical Advancement – Of all CMS available today, Drupal has the most advanced technology. It does not require a lot of system resources, which eliminates the need for constant upgrades when website traffic and requirements increase

- Performance – Web pages created with Drupal load more quickly than most other pages created with a different platform. These also have faster response times compared to ones made with WordPress or Joomla.

- Customization – Customizing is easy with Drupal using a lot of plug-ins and themes, as well a host of other options for configuration. For those who have enough knowledge on programming, the root files can also be edited. These give Drupal the highest flexibility among the top performing CMS.

- Free – Software for Drupal can be downloaded for free. it can be installed into your own web hosting server, too. However, Drupal does not offer web hosting on its servers. You should have a web host ready in order for the site to run. Also, you should already have a domain name before you use Drupal.

Even with its magnificent advantages, there are a few difficulties that might be encountered by the owner of the website, such as:

- Need for technical knowledge – This does not mean advanced level, but at least the basic knowledge on error message troubleshooting and identification of coding problems.

- Need for technical support – Additional technical support may be necessary when the website goes beyond the basic small business or blog. This may require you to hire someone to do the technical stuff if you are not at a higher level of knowledge when it comes to things like these. Drupal requires in depth knowledge on technology and programming.

Joomla

This is often considered by many as the compromise between the 2 more popular CMS platforms namely, Drupal and WordPress. It runs smoothly, without hitch, on a large number of web servers. Users do not need to have the same technical expertise required by Drupal. However, users still get to enjoy a few extra features. There are a lot of themes and plug-ins to choose from, allowing users to customize their websites' function and design.

Advantages of using Joomla include the following:

- Social Network – The Joomla platform allows for fast and easy creation of social networks. This is considered as the biggest advantage that Joomla offers. Most websites would depend heavily on a good social network, such as those with products and services to sell or promote.

- Commerce – Setting up online stores is easy and simple with Joomla. This platform has more native support for the needs of ecommerce websites compared to Drupal and WordPress.

- Simple – Joomla is not very technical compared to Drupal. It is actually the middle ground, with the ease of use of WordPress and the power of Drupal's technology.

- Help Portal – Joomla platform has a help portal where users can ask questions about using Joomla and get some technical support. However, it isn't as extensive or fast compared to the support pages of WordPress but is cheaper and quicker than that of Drupal.

- Free – This is a free website building platform.

Free Website Creation

Sites like Wix and Weebly offer free website creation. These may look great because of the ease of use. However, most experts recommend NOT using these for the following main reasons:

- No control over the website – Websites created through these are hosted on another web host, registered under the name of the website and not you. That is, if you make a website, say, on Weebly, your website will be hosted by a separate web host, under Weebly's name and not yours. This means that Weebly will have sole control over your site. Without prior notice, they can easily delete your site or implement any changes.

- Limited function and poor design – These offer very limited themes and/or templates. And more likely, you will be sharing the same theme with a number of websites. There is less customizability of the features and you won't be able to make adjustments to suit your needs and preferences.

- Additional fees – Most of these would require additional fees if you want to have your own domain name or more bandwidth or space.

INSTALLING THE PLATFORM

Once you have chosen and installed your platform, you will now be able to get right into website creation. Here are the steps:

Theme and Layout

Once the platform is installed, you will get a clean and very basic site. When using WordPress, you would have to log in to the dashboard. Here, you will be able to choose from several themes and start building your site.

When choosing themes, it should fit right into what your website's overall topic is. Search through the various themes and when you find what you want, click the "Install" button and then "Activate". Choosing the theme may take some time. Patience would eventually lead to the perfect one for you. Themes can be changed as often as you want. When you do, your previous posts, content and pages won't be deleted. If you want the theme to work when the site is accessed through mobile phones, use the keyword "responsive" when you are searching for themes.

Contents and New Pages

Time to create the content once the theme is installed. You can add information, articles, links and images. You can also create multiple pages, such as the Home page, About Us, FAQ, Support page, etc.

Web Pages

To create new pages in WordPress, follow these steps:

- Log in to the dashboard

- Click **Pages**

- Select the option "**Add New**"

- If the pages are to appear on the menu bar of the website, go to the option "**Appearance**", select "**Menus**" then add the new pages to the list.

Posts

This feature enables people to post blogs or comments to your website. To enable this, add "Blog" or "Comment" to your menu bar. Follow these steps:

- Go to "**Posts**" and select "**Categories**" to create e new category on your menu bar.

- Go to "**Posts**" and select "**Add New**" if you want to enable the creation of blog posts. Add the right category from the list for better organization.

Tweaking the website

You can further customize your website by adding widgets and comments. You can also change the title of your website, as well as its tagline.

Tagline and Title

To change these, click "**Settings**" and choose "**General**". You will be given a form to fill up, where you input the "Site Title" and "Tagline".

Comments for pages and posts

You can enable or disable posting comments on your website. To do this:

- Choose "**Screen Options**" when creating a new web page. Choose "**Discussion**". A box will appear, showing the option "**Allow Comments**". Untick the box if you don't want comments. Tick it if you want visitors to leave comments.

If you want the default for all new pages either to enable or disable the comments, follow these:

- Click "**Settings**" and choose "**Discussions**". Tick or untick the options according to your preference.

Front page

If you want the front page of your website to be static, follow these steps:

- Click "**Settings**"

- Choose "**Reading**" and then choose the particular page you want to be static.

DESIGNING A WEBPAGE

Some people create the web page after setting up their websites. They would just click certain options in the dashboard and menus to create the different pages. Some have to use special software to create a new web page.

The design is dependent on your preference, your target visitors and the type of product you want to place in the webpage. For most, thinking of the concept is the hardest step to take. Most people would spend long precious days just thinking of the concept. It is advisable to just start with an idea and get something out there. It isn't expected that the 1st design would immediately catch on and drive enough traffic to the website. The point is to put up the webpage as soon as possible. Waiting too long would mean losing a good number of potential visitors. There is always time as well as opportunities to fine-tune the design once the page is already up.

Web editors help in creating the web design. One popular web editor for newbies in webpage design is WYSIWIG or What You See Is What You Get. These editors allow for visual design without requiring tinkering with technical details of the design. These work much like regular word processors where users just input what they want and change it into preferred design.

There are also free and commercial web editors available. One example is the Dreamweaver which is one of the most recommended by a lot of web experts.

6 SETTING UP A BLOG

A blog or weblog is a type of website, which is designed to maintain ongoing or continuous updates or chronicling of certain topics. It is much like a diary where commentaries and links are constantly added to the website. These blogs or posts are added and arranged in reverse chronological order. Topics range from personal topics (e.g., entries about one's journeys, etc.) to politics and health.

Create a Blog

Creating a blog includes the following steps:

1. **Think of a topic.**

   This is the most crucial part. The topic would dictate how the website would look like and what features should the website contain.

2. **Decide on the platform.**

   Most blogging platforms use WordPress because of its ease of use and its free availability. This platform also allows other people to post comments or share your blog on other websites or on social networking sites.

   Beware of using other free blog creation sites like tumblr.com and blogger.com. These work much like other free website platforms where the domain is not yours, you have no full control, etc. Also, these sites do not allow you to earn money through your blogs (which can be a bummer if your blog catches on and you get some good money-making opportunities).

Some choose to create their own blog domain, pretty much like creating any other type of website.

3. Choose a domain and webhost.

    This step is similar to the previously discussed steps in creating a website.

Setting up a Blog with WordPress

This platform is the most popular among blog building platforms. This is also the most reliable and flexible, with can cater to all your present and future needs. to set up:

- Get a blog domain name and a web host from WebHostingHub. This has a very easy to follow set-up process that beginners find convenient to work with. This will require a small fee for the domain name that would be exclusive for your use.

- Next, check the "WHOIS Privacy". This is not that important but if you choose not to share your name to viewers of your blog, you can tick this box.

- Fill the fields that require your personal information. This step is important to make sure that your transaction is kept confidential.

- Install WordPress after you have obtained your domain and verified your hosting account. You will receive instructions and an AMP log in information. AMP is Account Management Portal).

- Log in to the **AMP Home** to start blog installation.

- Click "**Your Account**" then select "**Install popular software**"

- Select "**WordPress software**"

- A table will open where you will choose from different blogging platforms. Choose WordPress (or other platforms if you want)

- Place the title of your blog under *Site name*.

- Place a short description of your blog under *Site Description*.

- Change the admin username and key in a password.

- You can now start blogging.

7 CONCLUSION

Thank you again for buying this book!

I hope this book was able to help you to make your own website in no time. The tips and tricks here are to help you find out the steps you need to take in order to make the best decision when making your own website. As you have seen, some sites would give attractive offers but may not benefit you much in the long run.

The next step is to set up your own website today and enjoy the rewards that the Internet can give you.

Finally, if you enjoyed this book, please take the time to share your thoughts and post a review on Amazon. It'd be greatly appreciated!

Thank you and good luck!

8 PREVIEW OF: MOBILE APPS - HOW TO MAKE THEM, SELL THEM, AND HAVE FUN DOING IT!

Chapter 1: Why Apps?

Mobile phones are necessary in the daily lives of Americans. Only a handful of people do not have one in their pockets. And these devices have become excellent marketing devices as well.

The uses of mobile phones today are no longer limited to allowing people to connect with each other. Regular smartphones are now integrated with cameras, online connectivity, GPS, and operating systems that can run multitude of programs or apps – as they are known to the masses.

The cellphone has experienced rapid development during the past few years, so much so that it seems that the industry plans to deviate from Moore's Law – a law that guides hardware manufacturers on how fast they should release an updated or a more powerful device. And it can be attributed to the fierce competition between mobile phone manufacturers.

With all those in mind, it is only logical for an aspiring entrepreneur to join the fray. The mobile phone industry IS a huge cash cow. There are a lot of people that have smart phones, and those who will join the cellphone industry will have a chance earning a windfall because of a large and thriving target market. What's even better is that your target market will not always be limited to a certain geographical region; you could tap markets outside the United States as well.

But how exactly can a newbie entrepreneur enter the industry and start making a profit? You cannot just create a new brand of mobile phone. It will require a huge sum of money. And it is almost impossible to compete with the big guys, Samsung and Apple.

The answer is in apps development. And this book will help and guide you find success in the mobile development industry.

So why should you invest in app development, exactly?

First of all, they are a digital product. You can sell them across the globe without worrying about dealing with keeping inventory, couriers and sending packages. Just upload the app you want to sell in an online store, promote them, and wait for people to buy and download it.

Second, the market is still young. Certain niches may be saturated, but there is always room for one more. You can discover new niches or present apps that are way better than what are currently in the market. You can always opt to prevent fighting head on with competitors any time you want.

Remember, apps are digital tools that are designed to solve problems or to entertain. There are tons of problems you can choose to provide solutions by selling an app. There are also more problems than app developers in the world. In addition, people are always looking for new sources of entertainment; you can create games or other entertaining apps if you want.

An example of saturated app market is the one for mobile text editors. If you check an app store and look for text editors, you will find a lot of them.

It is advisable to avoid that market. Unless you can offer a better text editor, then do it. But there is a large chance that you can't provide one.

Lastly, you can create the app yourself. You might think that those people who graduated studying computer programming are the only ones that can create apps. However, with the help of online app development platforms, even those who are capable of dragging and dropping icons on their desktop can develop apps and sell them in the online market.

9 CHECK OUT THE OTHER BOOKS BY ME

Below you'll find some of my other popular books that are popular on Amazon and Kindle as well. These are the titles of them which can be found by going to www.Amazon.com and typing Malcolm Rockwood into the search bar.

Don't forget to visit my Facebook Author Page: Malcolm Rockwood

Language Learning - An Introduction to Learning a New Language

Interview - How to Talk, Dress, and Earn your Dream Job!

Let's Buy a House! - The In's and Out's to Know for a First Time Home Buyer

United States Navy Boot Camp - The Complete Survival Guide for the

Website Building: How to Build your Own Website and Blog to Perfection!

Worst Eight Weeks of your Life!

Navy Life - How to Make the Transition from Civilian Life to Military Service!

Leaving the Navy - Things to Consider when Leaving the Navy and How to Join the Rest of the World!

Pet Ownership - Everything You Need to Know to Become Your Pet's Dearest Human.

Infidelity - Why it Happens, How to Heal, and How to Rebuild your Life.

Dealing With Difficult People - How to Deal with A-holes at Work, at Home, and at Life

Earthships: An introduction to Earthships and How to Achieve Sustainable Living

Mobile Apps- How to make them, sell them, and have fun doing it!

Roommates - The Guide to Sharing Space and Being Happy!

Website Building: How to Build your Own Website and Blog to Perfection!

The Dating Game - Find Out the Secrets to Better Dating and Finding your Perfect Partner!

Intimacy - How to Ignite your Love Life Emotionally, Sexually, and How to Bring Back the Fire!

Get Out of Debt - The Strategy Guide to Getting Out of Debt and How to Stay That Way!

Start your Own Business - How to Get Started Being your Own Boss!

Off Grid Living - Solar, Wind and Other Free Means to Achieve Sustainability

ABOUT THE AUTHOR

Born in Texas and raised all over the country Malcolm Rockwood never stayed in one place for long. After moving from Texas to New Mexico and then back to Texas he attended high school in Naples Florida. During college he made the leap and joined the United States Navy where he saw the world. After serving six years he left the United States Navy honorably but took a lot from the United States Navy with him to include his wanderlust. He continues to travel the world seeking things he doesn't know but understands he will know when he sees it.

He currently resides in the state of Washington